BEAUTIFUL
MINDS
ANONYMOUS
NAUSICAA / 2015

(a book of poems)

Printed in the United States of America

First Printing, 2015

ISBN: 978-1-329-29094-5

Lulu.com Self-Publishing
Raleigh, North Carolina, United States

BeautifulMindsAnonymous.wordpress.com

for my one true love

(diamonds in our pockets)

maybe our obsessive numbering of things
has distracted us.
when, all this time,
we have all been carrying
diamonds in our pockets...

(angel in jeans and a t-shirt)

i'm an angel in jeans and a t-shirt
i stand up proud although i've been hurt
i learned to laugh wide
i learned to cry and not hide
i learned to smile and not be shy
regret no more
opened the door to beautiful shores

(past midnight)

past midnight;
ghosts want to come out
dreams beckon me loudly
dreams are always
stronger than ghosts
or so i tell myself
deep into the night

(don't fade away)

and, once again,
i remain in a state of awe.
it is perfectly normal
yet out of this world.
"don't fade away...."
i whisper to myself
and then i remember:
it's not even up to me....

(nothingness)

it's late
it's half past
nothingness
a beautiful moment
where nothing exists
and anything
is
possible

(a poem can change the world)

it has been a while and i have missed my words.

my words are my home.

i am boundless,

limitless,

free.

my words are the most beautiful thing i possess.

because my words tell me

that a poem can change the world;

and i believe them.

(i am greater than "me")

i'm smarter than you think
i'm more vast and capable than you know
brighter than you can perceive
more elegant and graceful than you've seen
wiser than you give me credit for
more generous than you knew existed
more complex than your perception of me
more alive than your eyes can handle
i'm greater than "me"
i am free and abundant
beyond expectations and infiltrations
i'm in solitude yet connected to all that is
i won't stop
until the blissness i was birthed in emerges...

(i will love)

i will live
[i will love]
i will live
[i will love]
i will live
[i will love]
i will live
[i will love]
... and it will be beautiful;

(being real)

i am addicted to
being real
obsessed with undressing
the truth
consoled by hope in humanity
lost inside my quest for me
somewhere you feel it too
somehow i will know you
through these words
through this moment
there is only one thinker

(where are you?)

where are you?
are you thinking of me too?
soft, familiar gasps
please be real
i've looked for you my whole life

(everlasting)

beautiful dreams
everlasting
in my depths
that's where i found you
your arms around me fiercely

(dwell in dreams)

i dwell in dreams
my true home is
traced by whispers
the mud on my face
doesn't exist in my world
which is
vast
eloquent
poetic
and deeper than the ocean's heart

(silence)

i don't say much
i let my actions be my voice

(birds)

falling
asleep
to
birds
chirping--
that's my kind of madness

(i believe)

i believe
that every dream
sincerely
wants to be born

(beautiful minds)

who are we
when we're alone?
who are we
when no one's home?
inside of you
in spite of you
we're the beautiful minds
we're the beautiful minds
we're the beautiful minds
with the beautiful souls

(cocoon)

"this cocoon is stifling,"
said
every
butterfly
that ever
was

(what's in a name?)

i don't know which i dislike being called more:
sweet names
or
bad names
even my name has a facade to it;
i think i prefer
"hey you--"
with a warm gaze of knowing
who
i
really
am

(love)

love...
...burns in my chest
...burns out of my gut
...burns an open trail
to the most beautiful things
i can't
yet
fathom

(wild floods of time)

no one wants to give up on love
we are all forced to
by wild floods of time
and
twisted fates
that crashed upon us
and
tore our love away

(the perfect wave)

whether dragged by the undertow,
or surfing the synchronicities
i still live for the perfect wave
and the chance to sincerely exclaim,
"kowabunga!"

(deep chaos)

believe in me,
i whisper--
dream of me,
i surrender--
laugh with me,
i dare you--
i crave the deep chaos within you...

(sincerity ?)

sincerity?
you never really know
who is flattering you
and who would follow
you fiercely
into the deepest
caves of your soul

(emerge)

let me emerge
i've existed submerged
laughs, cries--
feelings that surge
definitive vows
blessed and renewed
i pull out these words;
the heart
from
my
chest

(roadtrip)

on an open road
friends stacked high
our favorite music plays
we drive for miles
at twilight
we build fires
and share secrets
all but one sleep
we dream
to the soft sounds
of a guitar
i wake up at dawn;
how can it get any better than this?

(ghosts)

we live in a time
where we mourn the living
we know where their ghost lives
but force ourselves
not to go there--
an expensive gift
of the modern era

(no title)

i have no title
is that ok?
that i have an unusual mix
of interests and ideas?
that i could change my mind
based on my own intelligent perception?
that i could be anyone or anything or anywhere?
please stop trying to define me
you won't succeed

(angels)

we fight;
we writhe--
we break broken bones
and take up residence
in ridiculous homes.
we contemplate
the impossible
wander into the improbable
release miracles into thin air
while letting angels
play with our hair....

(forever)

in the twenty first century
we learned
that forever
could be broken
again
and again
and again...

(once)

once
you are done feeling bad
and you decide
time is limited
and you want to use it
on things that matter
that's the day
you will see things
you could never see
before

(little known deep thinkers)

i like to find
little known deep thinkers
and little known quotes
by great minds
and the poetry
inside everyone
everyone has beautiful depth
some of us
look for it where ever we go

(beautiful soul)

what is more beautiful
than a soul
who's been locked up
finally
coming out to play?

(wild roses)

and
wild roses
grew
where
you
left
thorns

(pay attention)

are you paying attention?
there is a trend happening
it is beautiful
it is rare
souls seeking truth
enriching their minds
upholding the value
of truthful pondering
perhaps
the greatest trend
ever to be

(lost green eyes)

she said:
"i've lost a thing or two in this life,"
but later i found out
that she had lost a lot more
i wanted to tell her
that it was ok
and
that i would be there,
but the words
got caught in my throat
when i gazed into her
lost
green
eyes...

(freestyle session)

the best way to be
is fiercely in the moment--
spontaneous
freestyle
session;
that is life

(palaces)

maybe it appears
i have done nothing
all these years
but
you have no idea
how many palaces i have built
in my mind

(love is never hard)

"is it possible,"
she asked,
"to love so hard
that you make
all things right
in the world?"
"no,"
he said softly,
"because
love
is never hard."

(sun scorched roads)

they travelled for days
sun scorched roads
and quick stop food
the feeling of saltwater
still on her skin
she rolled down her window
and let the wind
make her new

(strike the moment)

you don't need to
"wait" for the moment to
"strike"
the moment is right there...
waiting for
"you" to strike
"it"

(eyes)

eyes shut
deep breaths
let the dreams overflow
wisdom resonates
feelings obliterate
shreds of eloquent masquerades
chaos endures
silence prevails
the beauty that blazes
a wide open trail

(great minds)

when great minds collide
fireworks light up
the collective mind's sky

(the power of words)

the power of words;
always remember
the power
of
your
words.

(he was not you)

he loved me
like i wanted to be loved
but he
was not you

(ninja)

one day,
she thought to herself,
"enough."
that was the day
she became a ninja
and disappeared
in a very ninja fashion

(life)

life
predicts
moments
without
knowing
what
the
next
line
will
be.

(home on the horizon)

there is a home
on the horizon
it's where you are
waiting for me
i have been
walking day and night
to get to you
until then
feel me in the sunshine
and remember that
it's always been you

(she loved herself)

and she loved herself
and he knew it
and he couldn't bear the thought of it
he wanted
all of her love
all to himself

(hunter)

i am a hunter;
i hunt miracles
and specs of gold
in disasters
i hunt sunshine
and wisdom
within senseless situations
and when i capture that which i hunt--
i scatter them like seeds across
a fertile land:
my heart.

(forever)

forever was all we had;
and forever
was just a moment.

(nuclear winter)

she was sweet sunshine
with storms in her eyes
"i hope he survives
my nuclear winter,"
she whispered.

(impossible)

we are the dreams
that the impossible
contemplates

(center)

and then
it was time
to come back
to center--
center stage,
self-centered, indulgence
just center:
the heart of the soul.

(we laughed)

we laughed so hard
under the stars
that everything melted--
except for that moment.

(last words)

if these
were my last words
i would use them
to remind you
to smile again

(sometimes)

sometimes
i like to look into
memories that never were
inside a life that never was
it makes me happy
to think
that in that parallel world
you were real
and if i feel it enough
i just may wake up with you

(revolutions of thought)

we give home to the
weary,
orphaned
feelings
in
the
communism
of positive thinking.
it's beautiful
to lift the oppression
of how we "should" feel
and spark our own
revolutions of thought

(hardest thing to hear)

the hardest thing to hear
is what someone
does
not
say

(no one at all)

she wore mostly black
but she was not goth
wearing shirts inside out
she rejected labels
and believed in her own solitude
she was style-less
advocating her freedom
to be no one at all

(ignite)

don't wait to be granted permission--
you must
ignite
the
raging
fire
within

(moonbeams and bones)

some of us write about
the stars--
as we are lying in gutters
some of us bask in
moonbeams--
as we are collecting bones

(early bird songs)

the blanket of
early bird songs
surrounds any trace
of
feeling alone

(what matters)

"what matters?"
i asked myself this one day;
and it liberated
a flock of bad dreams
from my house of thought

(she)

she
was
inhumanely
strong
holding
together
iron
walls
with simple
thread and needle

(secret euphoria)

being understood:
the secret euphoria
for my soul

(nothing)

once upon a time,
we did nothing;
it was brilliant.

(freedom)

freedom is a wild beast
not once stopping to wonder
if it's been copyrighted

(my muse)

you drank in my words
like sweet wine;
you didn't need them to
survive,
but you craved them
like they were your sustenance.
and you, my muse--
i needed you
in the same way.

(stand up)

don't let them break you
there is a magic deep inside
beneath the weakness
beneath the pain
now, stand up;
the universe is calling
your name

(loving her madness)

if she tells you she's crazy; believe her.
don't promise her you can handle it
believe me--you can't
don't be charmed by her madness
instead, love it for the beast that it is
don't try to tame it either
because you will only hurt both of you
just gaze at her tenderly
ask her how she heals
and what she needs you to do
because she may never heal
but if she does
it will be because someone held her hand
through her darkest of nights
without looking away....

(reality)

    enter: reality.
a stark, cloaked figure with weapons for eyes
derailing the balance between
that which you thought to be true
and that which haunts you.
    neither is true.
instead, something unexpected and brave
fearless in the unshaped
commencement of thought
the very vast and elegant:
    i am
in the end, all things weave like thunderclouds
black, white, grey, with rainbows that beckon
you learn the last thing there is to know
the wild perpetual beauty
    it shall never be defined

(a million poems)

a million poems
running through my head
if i don't write them down
they'll drive me mad instead

(you)

you
delightful you
swimming in my bones you
wrapped around me you
i gaze upon you like mountains at fall
with color and grace
deep feeling
wound up beauty
braided into me
you
the dreamer
you
the seer
do you see me too?
i like to think so
as the wind sails me back to you....

(profound)

dress it up
dress it down
its essence remains
brave and profound
brilliant style
and eloquent grace
never can it be
lost or misplaced
recognizing visions
wild and free
the mark on my heart
returns back to me

(more fierce)

I'll always have
wild hair
and a blunt tongue
clothes scattered about
untamed eyes
and the irresistible
urge to attempt
something beautiful
they tried to box me up
but all they did
was make me more fierce

(endless gaze)

can you feel it?
the wind is here
she pulls on you softly
unraveling you eloquently
bright waves of forever
shining upon
your endless gaze

(bare hands)

there
is no
preparation
but
the
bare hands you possess

(breathing words)

some write for hobby
some for pleasure
i am looking for souls
who write like they breathe
who have a pure relationship
with words
who feel bliss
with a pen and open journal
because we who live to write
simply cannot stop writing
cursed with a blessing
of a gift
restlessness, surrender,
write, write, write

(orphaned feelings)

we adopt orphaned feelings
from
communist optimist regimes
which is the reason
why
poetry feels like home

(the secret of the woman on the run)

deep inside the depths that prevail,

lies a beautiful woman wearing a veil,

the veil is thick but her eyes are vast,

she knows you well,

your questioning heart remembers her fast,

this woman wears black and she beckons you--

and try as you might you cannot get through;

for she calls you in the most alluring of ways--

with truths that burn through you

for all of your days,

she wears a veil but her eyes tell all,

she hands you a letter with secrets and all,

she hands you this letter

in the most urgent of ways,

she hugs you tightly as the daffodils sway,

she shares her message that haunts you for years,

its message provokes your deepest of fears;

and try as you might, you tell no one--

and you live with the secret

of the woman on the run....

(alchemist)

there is a room in my mind
what my heart will not enter
it remains shut, bolted and nailed
cemented over and forgotten
but this room in my mind
screams with silence
it endures the concrete
ad nudges to me to explore it once again--
because in this room lives an alchemist,
and over the years,
it has filled up with gold.

(kings)

i know.
there is "only so much time in the day"
but make sure you give people the time of day
especially the lost, sick and broken ones
the ones you are most likely to ignore
are often masters in disguise
wealthy beyond what you can understand
and more beautiful than you can imagine
maybe they are undercover kings
testing to see what your heart is made of

(angel's caravan)

i've seen your pain
i've seen your struggle
i've watched your eyes grow dim
when you thought no one was looking
i recognize the beauty that you are
i know the impossible dream you chase
i live in the spaces of your dreams
i am vast awareness
i am the poet behind the poet's eyes
i know that you long for more
i know how you mourn
and are still mourning
dreams that could not be
i dance in the sweetness you possess
i revel in the beautiful spaces yet to be
i am the dreamers dream
lost
liberated
unmade
evolving
free...
one day,
you will find me lost upon an angel's caravan
singing symphonies collected for you

(music)

the music of my soul
shakes alive
the rhythm
of
my
heart

(madness gazing)

some people warn against
gazing in to the madness
but
i find
gazing into the madness
to be the only cure
for the madness itself

(stand ground)

it requires
great character
to stand ground
against
that which wants to
knock you out

(rare breed)

i have come to learn
that those of us
who stop short
of hurtful language
who see the futility
in fighting against
inevitability
and choose to focus
on the beautiful things;
are a rare breed indeed.

(this era)

i love this era;
we have all become
photographers
writers
and
deep thinkers
i believe
that future generations
will thank us for that

(we want our freedom back)

we have the right to remain anonymous
anything we say or do can remain
as an idea in the space of time
we do not owe anyone details of our life
we have a right to protect ourselves
from bullies, stalkers and other "anonymous"
who hide for the purpose of doing harm
we do not hide
but, rather, express a matter of principle
very simply put:
we want our freedom back

(late night)

late night,
black sky--
among the darkened
passersby;
mind hallucinates;
wisdom resuscitates--
eyes follow the lights
the cold
and tender
melancholic
sights

(freedom in our bones)

we continue on
with stars in our eyes
with food for our thoughts
with freedom
in
our
bones

(be brave)

there are some of us who feel so strongly
that we get lost inside our own feelings
and all things of this world
cannot bring us back
and only beautiful dreams
can bring back the light in our eyes
as we reach for things already forgotten...
to those people, i say only this:
be brave.

(affinity)

he adored her--
especially in those moments;
there, in the field--
when the sky
had turned a deep shade of twilight
and the wind spoke
their language:
affinity

(vivid creations)

do not
worry
of what has passed
wake up fresh
in the dream of
right now;
magnificent
hyper
truth
of vivid
creations

(come)

come;
let us laugh
and play
unravel our cares
into the sunset glare
let us love deeply
and speak sweetly
and when the morning comes
let us do it all over again

(the land of poetry)

in the land of poetry
we learn to dance free
removing shackles
accepting scars
redefining hope
undressing pride
and letting the
brilliance of our hearts
overtake us

(kaleidoscope)

my mind is a mixed up kaleidoscope
of old photos and broken wishes
it does not discriminate
all flood in
all the time
and I was born with an impeccable memory.
and I cannot forget
and so, instead,
i make art with these shards
stuck on my heart...

(you deserve more)

you deserve more.
you are worth more.
you.
yes, you.
you deserve someone who knows your worth
and proves it every day.
you deserve someone who asks themselves
what they can do for your heart, and does it.
you deserve a wild hearted soul
who sweeps you away into special dreams
you could not imagine.
you deserve a kind hearted spirit who lets you love
like you could never fathom.
you deserve real, consistent,
unwavering, free flowing love.
you deserve to be cherished
and to be someone's "dream come true".
you deserve to question everything
and hold out for the one you are sure about.
you deserve this and so much more.
you deserve to be loved.
not just because it is your destiny;
but because someone out there
is specifically and desperately seeking you.

(closest thing to home)

what i write
is unscripted
uninterrupted
undefined
unedited
in the moment
freestyle
free flowing
free throughout
expression.
it is the closest thing
to "home" i know.

(there is no "normal")

there is no "normal"
there are only created moments
visions, manifested
things we wish we did better
things we wish we didn't do at all
and when it all comes back to you
normal is just a distraction
for the confusion it creates
while contemplating it

(twice as hard)

and when he loved her
she loved him back
twice as hard
because that was just the way she loved

("when?")

"when?"
she asked, shakily.
"when will you realize that you are truly loved?"
he looked in the distance for a long time.
his eyes glazed with old tears.
"probably during my last breaths."
his voice was lost in the distance.
she wrapped her arms around him
and squeezed him into her heart.
"you are so foolish,"
she whispered, between sobbing breaths.

(stunningly beautiful)

and when
you put down
all the layers
of your pretentious self
an awkwardness emerged
which could only be described
as
stunningly beautiful.

(unlimited dreaming)

we are
only as limited
as the dreams
we feel good enough for

(innocently reckless)

she had become
innocently reckless
without meaning to
and try as she may
she could not seem to
throw the caution
from the wind
back into her world

(mirrors)

mirrors
at dawn
facing each other
shall bend in time
facing away
shall reflect in echoes
around
the
earth

(time before time)

there are beautiful things
which remain hidden
inside your deepest nostalgia
feel them--
nostalgia
for a time before time

(brave hearts)

on this journey
i have found beautiful minds
those who, simply put,
"get it"--
understanding the ineffable
pieces of my soul
and so, i sit in gratitude
that such connections happen
in awe of all who have come
to brave their hearts
in this wide open night

(i promise)

i promise
to be brave
to reveal my heart
knowing that shall
keep me safe
i vow to dig deeper
i *will* emerge these depths
into thin air
they *will* glow and shine
pulsate and call out
into the
wilderness of my heart

(justice)

and their cries
will not go in vain
it will be written
it will be told
there shall be justice
and their tears
will not be forgotten
and the monsters
that attack defenseless innocents
shall be remembered
for the monsters
that
they
are

(she rose again)

she fell

she crashed

she broke

she cried

she crawled

she hurt

she surrendered

and then...

the rose again

(bright star)

hey
bright star
across the universe
who burned me once
you yearned for me once
you cried and moaned
who turned to stone
who knew me
loved me
you
i miss you

(distant dream)

distant dream in a far off land
wished for a hope beyond these hands
these hands, they are empty
but the can hold you--
with vastly alive colors and hues
and the ache that remembers
is the very same ache
that once held you
lost in a dream
with yellows and blues
me, with my heart
open in the wind--
which hardly recollects
the light-hearted things
and i do feel
like a skeleton of ghosts
that ache in my bones
which aches for me most

(words)

words can heal
words can kill
words can get inside you
like no one else will
beautiful words
are worst of all
they climb into your heart
and then make you fall
when those beautiful words
are just skin deep
those beautiful words
drown you in your sleep

(she wept)

and she wept
a storm-cloud
of box-shaped,
stifled
emotions
that revived themselves
in the open air
so she could breathe

(find my way home)

even though
my sails are tangled
and my compass has died
and the shore is
nowhere to be seen
even with storms raging
and no plan
i still know
i will find my way home
to you

(saltwater)

and when she released
her wet hair
into the wind--
she released sea shells,
dolphin cries
and the entire
ocean's soul
across cities
never touched by
saltwater.

(odd creature)

she was an odd creature;
she was the only one i knew
who could be a success-
while failing miserably

(rethink your ideals)

i'm not giving in
to your automatic ways
drown me in guilt
and chaotic craze
i will not go down
i will stand my ground
you will rethink your ideals
that abuse and hound

(assured grace)

and we went
on a quest
of creating homes
for wild,
feral,
undisclosed
feelings--
but never on our terms;
always with assured grace--
like you would with a wild beast...

(dreamlovers)

draw me in
and remember
how our love melted
into the sunshine
we are dreamlovers;
together in a dream,
for all of time--
remember my face,
find me--
i am already yours...

(losing everything)

like a cloud
entangled with the wind
i was pushed
further and further out
past my shores
past the ships in the distance
torn away from everything i had known
even from my very own self
i learned to sail
i learned to swim
i learned to fly...
losing everything
was the most beautiful thing
i had ever known

(free-falling)

my ultimate quest remained
freedom.
and I had found it by
free falling
trusting I had it in me to
fly.

(letters)

if you have done
all that you can do
remember that
there are letters
in the mail
bringing the news you seek
and they will read,
"help is on the way..."

(self love)

i am into self-love;
mind
body
soul
spirit
i learn from my mistakes
i embrace my flaws
i know who i am
and i adore me..
won't you join me?
adore the beautiful self
you are

(universes of thought)

there are infinite
universes
calling out to you
wishing to be picked
for your experience
tell me,
which one of those universes
will you choose
from the depths
of your imagination?

(anonymity)

there is a reason
for anonymity
it rests in the spaces
where
"i am..."
is just a story
and all that is
is yet to be discovered...

(full of song)

i love the way
 you tell me
broken tales
of things gone wrong
with a face so bright
and full of song

(bird of hope)

there is a bird that calls out
in the distance
its song is hope
its wings are wide
once, its wings were clipped
once, this bird was caged--
but not now;
now, this bird has learned to fly
and this bird
is a color so blue
that when it flies,
it disappears
against the blues of the skies

(treasures)

there are castles
in my brain
kingdoms
in my heart
and galaxies in my eyes
many have tried, but
no one can steal those treasures
away from me...

(being without power)

i lost my power in the storm
it was a total
and complete
outage
it was midnight
so i lit candles
and listened to the silence
the silence grew loud
and spoke to me
in all the ways
i could never hear before
when my home was flooded by light
and animation again,
i kept the lessons of the darkness safe inside
i would never forget
the beautiful depth
of being without power

(stars still dancing)

i want passion.
i want friendship.
i want late-night,
undefined,
intimate moments...
i want deep love--
i want real love--
the kind of love
that never lets you sleep;
but leaves you rested...
and when we wake up;
we wake up to the stars
still dancing from the night before

(born beautiful)

we are born beautiful
caged by circumstance
devoured by illusion
and starved by ignorance
but we are born beautiful
and at any time
we can rebirth
ourselves
...all over again.

(is human behavior natural?)

i don't believe in labels
i don't believe in judgments
digging deeper requires us to ask
is human behavior natural?

(HOPE)

and
H
O
P
E
emerged;
it swept up
the pieces
into a glass
jar
"i shall make
something
beautiful,"
hope said.

(warm-blooded affection)

i don't want
to be admired
from behind a glass wall
i want warm-blooded affection;
pull me in close
and whisper all the ways
you want to know me

(she could fly)

and on the days
she could not
even crawl--
she untied her dreams
and let the flock of inspiration
fly out of her mind's attic...
soon, she found herself amidst the flock of dreams,
flying to places she had never dreamed of...
and in those places,
she realized that she could no longer crawl;
she could fly...
she could fly!

(wild tales)

the paper gazes
right into my soul
soft
familiar
enchantment
of
all wild tales
pressing
to be told

("all in")

and
that was it;
love, in all its mad wisdom,
laid out--
dealing a raw deck
with no wild cards;
no, this time,
love was "all in";
this time--
she called their bluff
by the stars in their eyes.

(fertile soul)

once
she accepted less
and she
cut herself in half
cut herself in half
cut herself in half
and woke up alone
with a small corner
of herself left...
so she traded her scissors
for fertile soil
and harvested that corner
so she would bloom
and flourish
with fruit for all
and her wholeness sustained

(dreams bask)

we don't sleep anymore
here,
we only dream
and dreams never sleep
dreams bask
exhilarated
by their
own
essence

(what now)

i have decided to change my address--
from
"what if?"
to
"what now?"
...the view is much better.

(something magnificent)

yesterday
is another generation
today
is worth a million wishes
right now
is the most precious thing there is
tomorrow,
we may not be here--
but, in this moment,
something magnificent wants to be known...

(star athletes)

we are all star athletes
running our own marathon
for some of us,
the marathon is won
by simply
opening our eyes in the morning...

(unbroken, unashamed)

when you held me,
with your eyes
wept with midnight prayers,
and your emotions
melted apart and soft,
with your original face
finally revealed:
merciless and unrelenting--
my eyes closed
and i fell deeply into you
unbroken,
unashamed.

(I AM)

I AM ;
a powerful statement
which can
giveth
or
taketh away

(speaking your truth)

never fear
speaking your truth
those who understand
will thank you
and those who don't
are just afraid of
their own truth

(love me like a poem)

i want to be loved
as my poetry describes;
so, please,
do not take another step toward me
unless you love me
for the beautiful masterpiece that i am
because,
as my poetry describes,
i will love you twice as hard.

(untamed heart)

untamed heart
so wild and free
when you see with wild eyes
what do you see?
do you see the magic
un-spun,
un-won--
do you see the sound waves,
one by one?
do you see the lights
too bright for blind eyes?
you're and acquired taste;
wild
heart
in
me...

(take your time)

if you want love,
take your time...
know yourself
grow yourself
enjoy yourself
free yourself
be yourself
see yourself
in the end, you will find love;
your lover is waiting inside a secret room
of self acceptance
within your heart.

(give eyes for eyes)

an eye for an eye
leaves us eyeless, indeed!
did you ever think
of all those in need?
could you have done more
for those who bleed?
did you ever wonder
where you would be
without the kindness
of those who see?
an eye for an eye
yes, i agree--
give eyes for eyes
so we all can see

(diamonds and scars)

aren't you tired
of looking at these screens?
don't you want to "be"--
instead of living vicariously?
don't you want to see
the beauty that you are
when you
shine and rage
with
diamonds and scars?

(third world wonders)

i've been to suburbs
i've been to the ghetto
i've been to world class
second class
third world wonders
i've eaten meals with the indigenous
shared words with the prestigious
walked proud past soldiers in riot gear
moved through packs of wild dogs with no fear
i've carried my life in a backpack
i've lost everything again and again
among revolutionaries obsessed with style
but what is army green?
red stars?
anarchy?
it's just another fashion statement
if you ask me
i march only for truth
set wild and free

(vibrant brilliance)

i'm
going to
rage
with
vibrant
brilliance
and
wisdom
that melts all
ignorance
and pain

(spaces)

we will never work,
you and i--
you are a star gazer
and i am the sky;
you will look right at me
and not see a thing...
because,
while you are looking
for shiny
objects,
i am the spaces in between.

(let me know how it goes)

almost every problem
can be solved
by waking up early
if you don't believe me--
try it...
...let me know how it goes.

(ultimate freedom)

wonderful ideas
brilliant thoughts
beautiful contemplations
wise thinking
dreamful, breathtaking
passionate joy
depth
freedom
elation....
beautiful thinking:
our ultimate freedom

(owing approval)

the beauty of who i am
does not need approval--
the beauty of who i am
is its own approval.

(mind masterpieces)

these walls
are plentiful--
my mind makes
windows
and decorates
them with
masterpieces.

(eloquent reprise)

sleepy eyes
dream filled sighs
eloquent reprise
love grasps me wise
the liberation of freedom
undiscovered
mists
of
penitentiaries
canaries sing sweeter
than captive mercenaries
wild dances overflight
wisdom seeks;
ignorance fights...

("...hold on...")

there is a small,
silent voice in the midst of disaster--
it doesn't say much
but it hums sweetly
promises for a better day,
whispering:
"...hold on..."

(thunder of dreams)

"i will.
i will be that for you...
...the peace
within the storm
and the joy
buried by pain
the sun,
the moon,
and the ocean,"
...a voice said.
it sounded like
pen against paper
mixed with the
thunder of dreams.
this voice belonged
to my heart...

(secret elixir)

maybe one day
you will find
the secret elixir
of your own soul
and on that day
we can drink together
celebrating years lost
as battle wounds
and the promised land
who really did wish to be found

(never stop playing)

a message to youth:
be responsible
but
never
stop
playing;
there will be times
when only fun can save you.

("yes!")

right now
in the ripe precious
realm of possibility
dreams dance
with pieces of your heart
and,
if you listen closely,
the music that plays
is the sound of you saying:
"yes!"

(making my own way)

i'm not counting milestones;
i am a full tank of wonder
going full speed
all the way into eternity
past all roadways and maps--
i am making my own way

(love did reign)

the lost causes
of dwindled chances
knocked at her door--
she asked hope to remain
for just a little more--
dreams awakened
with him by her side...
hearts torn apart
souls opened wide...
a part of her
will forever remain
inside that day
where
love
did
reign...

(" no--")

" no--"
i spoke into
the freshly
painted sky.
"i will no longer
hold trauma in
these bones..."
the sky cleared;
it was a beautiful day.

(where your soul resides)

infinite realities

endless possibilities

boundless abilities

beyond what the eye

can

see

unmistakable

unshakeable

unfakeable

tides

...this is where

your soul

resides...

("--don't go;")

"--don't go;"
two words
so sweet as rain
and more powerful
than the laws of time
bringing back feelings lost
and realizations that sing
that love is our only master

(love still reigns)

love did reign
love does reign
love still reigns

(daughters of the sublime)

i fall
with random grace
in between
laughter's spell
and bewildering plot twists
somewhere in between,
i rendezvous
with daughters
of the sublime

(blindsided by life)

it's not your fault...
you got blindsided by life
uprooted by chaos
no one around you understood
you got pushed beyond your limits
and now, things are a little messy
so what?
you get to rest now--
it wasn't your fault
do you hear me?
it was out of your control
you are not to blame
you owe zero explanations
take stock of what matters
take a night off--
you will feel braver in the morning

(no shame)

do you think
she is ashamed
of who she is?
she's not--
don't lend her your shame
it's heavy,
and,
not even yours to carry.

(lost dreamers fly)

open those dreamers' eyes
let go
land softly
into the heart of this now
feel your path
open wide
feel the wisdom flying by
grab on and enjoy the ride--
this is how
lost dreamers fly...

(invisible race)

broken times
in a beautiful place
breathtaking stars
splatter in space
when she goes
she leaves not a trace
invisible
beautiful
deathless
race

(hand over your dying wishes)

wait--
before you sing praises
up and down love's boulevard
before you vow
one thousand forevers
into the last dreams of your world;
offer your scars,
offer your tears,
hand over your dying wishes--
that is when
hearts melt or separate...

(come here, go away)

i've got,
"come here, go away,"
i've got,
"i love you, but,
please don't stay."
i dreamt a dream
a dream of forever--
it cut me to pieces,
my insides were severed,
so come here, go away
if you know where i'm broken
you'll convince me to stay

(sandblast)

crisis is
an opportunity
to use your guts
to sandblast bullshit
stand up on shaky legs
and realize that
you can kick the habit
of limping
you have grown
new legs
a new mind
beyond oppression;
you will survive...

(the language of me)

" you didn't get it--"
she said, wiping rivers from her eyes.
"i needed something simple.
i needed something honest.
i wanted something real--
i am now lost in a corner of your mind
that segregates the language of me..."

(precious dreams)

as a baby
when you learn to walk
you fall,
again and again...
you do not surrender
to crawling--
you do not say,
"i guess i will just sit here."
you try and try and one day--you walk.
so tell me,
why have you given up
on those precious dreams
after just a few falls?

(resurrection)

her words were furious--
knocking down
telephone poles
and steeples
uprooting old, dried up roots--
swirling with cast-iron will
that did not stop
an endless tornado
with an eye
filled of resurrection

(wild again)

the air was new
the colors--
hues that hit the
eyes
with chaos and
delight--
something had changed.
something was different.
the movie screen of
"the past" had faded...
everything was wild again;

(curves)

he knew it then;
when her curves
became art
when her mannerisms
became poetry
when the look in her eyes
became sunsets
he knew he loved her more than any creature
he had ever known.
"my God, you are beautiful,"
he whispered into her soul.

(sweet air)

she drank in
sweet air
that hugged her lungs
like
lovers rediscovered

(the real you)

how would you behave
if you knew you were loved?
...that's the real you.

(wild adventure)

there are holes
in the fabric of time
that call and whisper
like a shadow
on a darkened alley
but their words are bright
they speak luminous songs
and if you should choose
to follow them
you are in for
a wild adventure indeed!

(too beautiful)

she had a language
she called it love
and, really,
this language was
too beautiful
for the naked eye...

(there are people)

there are people who feel that
their well-being and comfort ranks higher
than that of everyone else
they will scream, yell and protest
for their personal satisfaction
without regard
for civilized,
compassionate,
communication.
these people are commonly referred to
as "assholes".

(outside the lines)

i giggle
because that thing
you call
"impossible"
is really just
"never been done"
much like
flying,
photography,
and
coloring outside the lines
once were.

(hear our dreams)

sometimes,
the laughter and chaos,
buzz of the crowd,
glare of the screens,
drowns my mind...
can we go someplace quiet
to hear our dreams again?

(us)

wandering,
day and night,
bare feet over rough earth,
led by heart,
that cleared a path,
straight into
your soul;
with aching hearts,
tugging minds
we only followed
with brave longing,
belonging only to us.

("stand back!")

she has
a volcano in her heart
and lava in her veins
but
this is not her strength
her strength is
her ability to
hold back eruptions
and
the way she says
"stand back!"
when she finally does...

("breathe")

"breathe"
not all is lost.
look around--
the important stuff is here
the things that matter are with you
if only just your breath
breathe in, breathe out
with each breath,
you grow stronger;
you are FREE...

(a place i know)

inside my heart
is a place i know
where fields unravel
and valleys flow
inside this space
i dance with mountains
i drink sweet air
i speak with fountains
this space is my home
i go there often
i carry it with me
it's never forgotten
i will stay in this space
this space of mine
that awakens the sleeping
and gives sight to the blind

(dreaming petals)

let's scatter dreaming petals
across our path;
save nothing for tomorrow--
tomorrow does not exist...

(from dust to life)

and then
all the lost dreams
all the people missing
all the wishes made
emerged from
dust
to
life

(love for food)

she dwells in dreams
in the wilderness unseen
in star like gleams
in vast ocean scenes
he waits for her in the woods
a space beyond evil and good
designed to protect her beautiful mood
lilies throughout and love for food

(the miraculous)

the
miraculous
follows
the
brave

(poetic ingredients)

give me laughter
give me pain
this life is the sky
and i am the rain

(hearts gather)

"hearts gather where dreams shatter..."

(the news)

to those who follow the news:
just remember that headlines
are sales pitches
and what they are selling
ain't the truth...

(beautiful stories)

i have beautiful stories
locked up inside--
i write,
when i can no longer cry...

(deepest ache of my heart)

where do i find you now?
under my skin,
in my breath,
in the deepest ache of my heart?
in every step,
and every breeze,
and every sunlight that
dances upon my eye lashes?
i will find you--
in the shorelines of every lake
and every silver lining
of every cloud.
i will see you in every animal's eyes
and every touching moment
from every movie i will ever see.
i will feel you
in every mist
from every waterfall
and every puddle at springtime.
i will find you in my most beautiful emotions
i will always find you and see you there...

(black rose)

black rose--
what shall i disclose?
the rhythm of words,
or laughter of foes?
black rose--
dream me again,
find my hand,
be my friend...
black rose--
where are you now?
i once was your sunlight,
then, in blackness you drowned...

(that which carries me)

i am petals
lost on the wind
i have no home
except the breeze
i belong to that which carries me

(give and give)

we have this insane notion
that love means
"give and take"
when this is far from the truth
and describes a business transaction, not love;
love was never
"give and take"--
no, love has always been,
"give and give"

(man from my dreams)

if you happen to run into
the man from my dreams,
tell him i love him
with every wishbone
that's ever been...

(deepest eloquence)

she
believed
in
brave
beautiful
things
that danced
from the rooftops
of her soul's
deepest eloquence

(true brilliance)

it's as simple as this:
don't give one person
authority over you.
let many people know you
as you shine out
believe in yourself.
you will find those who believe in you
and leave behind critics
realizing they are isolated incidents
and never reflect
your true brilliance.

(hands)

open your eyes
open your mind
open your heart
and then,
open your hands to receive

(keep it on)

modesty is rebellion
in a world that shouts,
"take it off!"
darling,
be rebellious--
look them in the eye,
and,
keep it on.

(life wins)

life will always win;
stalked by chaos
hunted by death
enduring devastation..
life wins--
each second,
new life begins.

(fire's cousin)

he watched her anxiously
as she played with fire
not once stopping to think
that she was its cousin

(the moon's wail)

i am
the breath inside summer air
i am the tug inside your ribcage
i am the miracles not-yet-seen
i am the only love that's ever been
i am warmth in wintertime
i am the fragrant breeze in spring
i am freedom sprung up from earth
i am the sun's laughter
i am the moon's wail
i belong to no one
i live only in tales...

(i'm alive)

today
i woke up
inside the piece of my mind
where dreams are real...
i guess i didn't really wake up at all;
hold the alarm--i'm alive.

(the biggest lie)

the biggest lie we tell
is when we refer to ourselves as
"objective"--
we will never be objective,
and that's ok;
because we can be
aware,
loving, and
truthful--
which is worth much more
than mere objectivity...

(your best advocate)

your best advocate
is the one you never had to convince

(love your heart)

"follow your heart!"
we often hear
but to those whose hearts are lost
it becomes,
"find your heart;"
and to those whose hearts are poisoned.
it becomes,
"love your heart..."
your heart is a precious child
who needs a loving home first
and then, set it free and wild
and follow it fiercely
for it will lead your beyond your wildest dreams...

(golden shores)

i'll make it through
this dying night
my lungs are raw
my hands--respite
the look of angels
blue pale light
my knees are bruised
from crawling fights
on this day,
i, again,
drank from my reservoir
she pleaded,
"my friend,
there's nothing more--"
so i drank air instead and closed the door;
then swam through darkness
to golden shores...

(supernova)

each moment
holds the entire
universe
of who you are
and every second
is a supernova
waiting
to
happen

CONNECT

(email) BeautifulMindsAnonymous@gmail.com

(website) Beautifulmindsanonymous.wordpress.com

(facebook) Facebook.com/BeautifulMindsAnonymous

Facebook.com/NausicaaWritings

(instagram) Instagram.com/BeautifulMindsAnonymous

Made in the USA
Middletown, DE
16 August 2016